Life After College

Life After College

Lessons for Students in Transition

Will Keim

Chalice Press
St. Louis, Missouri

Art Director: Michael Dominguez

Cover design / illustration: John Spaulding

10 9 8 7 6 5 4 3 2 1   96 97 98 99 00

Library of Congress Cataloging-in-Publication Data

Keim, Will.

   Life after college: lessons for students in transition / Will Keim.

      p. cm.

   ISBN 0-8272-2125-8

     1. School-to-work transition—United States. 2. Success— United States.
     3. Ethics—United States. I. Title.

HD6278.U5K44 1996   95-52988
650.1—dc20   CIP

Printed in the United States of America

Acknowledgments

This book is dedicated to all of the students during the last ten yers who have said after graduation, "You know what I wish they had told me?" Life After College contains their insights and desires. In fact, this is the book I wish I had read before I left the University of the Pacific for Job #1.

Thanks to Lynn D.W. Lukow, Carol Wada, Dr. David Polk, R. Bruce Leamon, and Tricia Lott for their help with the original manuscript. Their friendship and professionalism have resulted in a valuable resource for students, parents, and professionals.

Special words of love and appreciation for my family—Donna, Christa, Samantha, J.J., and Hannah—for encouraging me toward the completion of this work. Without them, it would mean nothing. With them, everything! Thank you and I love you!

Good reading and a good Life After College

Will Keim, Ph.D.

Foreword

A great amount of time, effort, and resources are spent on the Freshman and New Student Orientation process and with good reason. Repeatedly studies have shown that an informative introduction and orientation to college life greatly enhances the chances for student success and retention. But what about life after college?

The transition between collegiate life and the workplace can be a challenging and validating experience for students who are prepared to make the journey. It can also be devastating for those who go blindly into the light many call the "real world." Life After College will prepare students for the transition between the campus and the boardroom or workplace.

A student's choices after graduation will largely be determined by what he or she learns in college and how prepared the student is to translate the university experience into a career or vocational path. Dr. Keim has lectured to over two million students and now shares his lessons with soon-to-be graduates. Life After College: Lessons for Students in Transition is an informative and hopeful book for students who want to get ready, set, and go!

Table of Contents

Introduction

LESSONS FOR STUDENTS IN TRANSITION

"Life is not a dress rehearsal."

Will Keim

This is a book for students who are completing one important phase of their lives and are moving into another one. It is a book about transition from "life in college" to "life after college." It is a collection of lessons filled with hope, insight, and specific suggestions about how to cope with change.

You may be going into the corporate world, the Peace Corps, graduate school, or moving home. Your age will vary as much as your life experiences. You are all on the verge of a transition between one experience and another and with all change comes a state of anxiety and expectation. The purpose of Life After College is to help you make the transition as smoothly as possible.

Lao Tzu wrote, "The journey of a thousand miles begins beneath your feet." It is time to step out into a new phase of living and direction. Welcome to Life After College! Your journey has just commenced.

"I was taught that the world had a lot of problems; that I could struggle and change them; that intellectual and material gifts brought the privilege and responsibility of sharing with others less fortunate; and that service is the rent each of us pays for living — the very purpose of life and not something you do in your spare time or after you have reached your personal goals."

Marian Wright Edelman

Life After College

There Is Life After College

*I*t usually hits most students the morning after graduation. "What in the world do I do now?" "Where should I go?" "What will I become?" For students going on to graduate school or with a job lined up these questions are less traumatic. Nevertheless, life as you knew it for four, five, six, or more years (depending on what plan you were on) is over. I hope you have created good memories.

Piaget said there is an anxiety phase that creates a readiness phase preceding achievement or attainment. This is your time to be concerned, to be anxious, to be excited; your feelings are normal and real. Now is the time to dream your dream and achieve your goals.

There is life after college and you will be all right there. You did not get to this point in your life by chance. You are a winner, a survivor, and you can adapt to change. The rest of your life is just beginning! The world has a lot of problems. You can struggle and change them.

> **You are a survivor. A winner. You made it!**
> ❖
> **Now comes the exciting part.**
> ❖
> **There is Life After College.**

A Moment for Reflection
Life After College

1. **Your assignment**: You have a paragraph in which to give an incoming freshman or new student the most important lesson you learned looking back at college. What would you say?

   _____

   _____

   _____

   _____

   _____

2. What is the most noticeable change you now see in yourself after life at the university?

   _____

   _____

   _____

   _____

   _____

3. **Checklist**: There are many things to accomplish before graduation and "Life After College." Refer to the Appendix at the end of the book and put a check in the box next to the items you have completed.

> "If you can walk you
> can dance. If you
> can talk you can
> sing."
>
> Zimbabwe Saying

The Last Lap

*Finish the Race with a Kick
(or a push or a roll!)*

*I*t is important to finish what you have started. The race through college is near its end and you must finish this race strongly and with pride. Why?

The momentum of your last term will carry you over into the next arena for your new race through graduate school or professional work. The strong finish will create a sense of pride in you and leave a good memory with your professors, mentors, and friends.

Simply put: You cannot arrive where you are going on the back of a fine stallion if you leave where you are on the back of an ass. Complete the assignment, go the distance, do what needs to be done. You are setting the banquet table now for the feast you will eat the rest of your life. Feast, not famine! Finish the last lap. You can dance and you can sing.

Build, do not burn, your bridges.

❖

Set the banquet table now for the feast of life.

❖

Finish the last lap!

A Moment for Reflection
The Last Lap

1. **Loose Ends**: I must complete the following assignments, projects, or tasks before I leave campus:

Task	Due Date	Completed (✓)
_____	_____	_____
_____	_____	_____
_____	_____	_____
_____	_____	_____
_____	_____	_____
_____	_____	_____
_____	_____	_____

2. The greatest fear or apprehension I have about leaving is:

_____

_____

_____

_____

3. The thing I am most looking forward to is:

_____

_____

_____

"To live is so startling
it leaves little time for
anything else."

Emily Dickinson

L E S S O N 3

Time Flies

*Whether You Are Having
a Good Time or Not*

*I*f graduation can teach you anything then it will teach you how fast time flies. Days pass like minutes. Years like weeks. You will be renting the cap and gown and wondering how you arrived there so fast.

Do not waste time. Do not pretend you will live forever and that you have an infinite amount of time to live. Do know that your days are numbered, your time is precious, and that you must squeeze each moment from each day.

The old women in my church tell me that the pace accelerates. How can this be? I just got going good and now I am forty. How old are you? Hasn't the journey been a quick one? Isn't life so startling? Live it...now!

Time is in warp drive, Mach 5.

❖

"Life is what happens to you while you are making other plans." Betty Talmedge

❖

Pay attention to the present; intention to the future.

A Moment for Reflection
Time Flies

1. Which of your collegiate years went the fastest? (✓) one:

☐ 1st   Why? _____

☐ 2nd   _____

☐ 3rd   _____

☐ 4th   _____

☐ 5th   _____

☐ +   _____

2. (a) If you are a traditionally-aged senior, what percentage of your life do you think you have lived?

   ✓ Answer: Approximately 25% or one quarter.

   (b) If you are a returning student or nontraditional in age, multiply your age times 365 and add the days since your last birthday. Subtract this from 25,000. How many days have you lived? How many days remain until 25,000?

   (c) Does this surprise you? _____

3. What are three things you can do to "slow down time"? (Think about daily activities.)

   (a) _____

   (b) _____

   (c) _____

> "The final test of a
> leader is that he
> leaves behind him
> in others the
> conviction and the
> will to carry on!"
>
> Walter Lippmann

LESSON 4

Burning Bridges

Nowhere to Run,
Nowhere to Hide

*O*nce I had a friend in graduate school that made a point of criticizing our university whenever he could at regional and national meetings. He burned a lot of bridges before he departed and left part of the academic community that spawned him charred in his wake.

Of what use is this? What good can come from this assault? If a university is terrible and I hold its diploma, then it would follow to an employer that I may be a worthless product of that questionable system. Who can be helped by this?

Speak kindly of your alma mater and others whenever you can. People forgive, but they do not forget. Do not burn bridges. You never know when you will have to retreat. The river is wide and deep and you'll need the bridges to get home. Leave behind others who think highly of you.

Build bridges.

❖

Leave your campus with integrity and dignity.

❖

Speak well of the institution that graduates you.

A Moment for Reflection
Burning Bridges

1. Have you ever said or done something you later regretted?

   What was it? _____

   _____

   To whom? _____

   _____

   Outcome? _____

   _____

2. What is the most positive statement you could make about your college/university?

   _____

   _____

   _____

   _____

3. What are some bridges or people with whom you need to do a little repair before you go?

PERSON	ACTION
_____	_____
_____	_____
_____	_____
_____	_____
_____	_____

> "There is nothing
> permanent except
> change."
>
> **Heraclitus**

Hello and Good-bye

Life in Full Circle

*a*s I have traveled around the world it has occurred to me that life is a seemingly never ending series of hellos and good-byes. Good-bye to my children, hello to my students. Good-bye to the United States, hello to Australia. And so it goes.

Soon you will say good-bye, for now, to your college friends. How will they remember you? Is there someone with whom you need to make peace? Are you afraid to say good-bye? Do not fear.

In my family we have ceased to say good-bye. I leave so often that the good-byes became too painful. We say, "See you soon." There are no guarantees, but this is our hope. Does this help you? I hope so! When you leave the campus you will say "good-bye" or "see you soon" many times. There are great opportunities to say "hello" just around the bend. Do not fear change for it is our only constant.

Life is a process, a journey, a circle. Hello and good-bye are part of the circle.

❖

"The only thing we have to fear is fear itself."
Franklin D. Roosevelt

❖

Nothing is constant except change.

A Moment for Reflection
Hello and Good-bye

1. **Write a brief hello letter** to your future employer or graduate school professor outlining your outstanding characteristics:

   _____

   _____

   _____

   _____

   _____

2. Write a draft of your "good-bye" or "see you soon" letter to someone at school who really matters to you:

   _____

   _____

   _____

   _____

   _____

3. Before I leave, I will bid farewell to:

   (a) _____

   (b) _____

   (c) _____

"Follow what you love!...Don't deign to ask what 'they' are looking for out there. Ask what you have inside. Follow not your interests, which change, but what you are and what you love, which will and should not change."

Georgie Anne Geyer

LESSON 6

What Now?

The Virtue of Patience

*M*any of you are coming to the end of one important phase of your life without any clue or concept about what you will do next. You are not alone. There are literally millions of students like you.

What now? Where to? When? How? So many questions, so much pressure, at a time that cries for clear thinking and patience. "Ask what you have inside." Look within and listen. What do you love and where can you best serve? These are the real questions.

"They" will always tell you what to do. Listen to "them" if they make sense. Otherwise, follow your heart. A little chaos is a good motivator. He or she who tolerates ambiguity best wins. Find your inner voice and get ready for the journey of your life!

Listen to your inner voice. Be calm and listen.

❖

A great tolerance for ambiguity is of great value in daily living.

❖

Follow your heart.

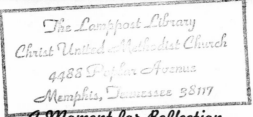
A Moment for Reflection
What Now?

1. If you could become anything in the world you wanted to be, what would you become?

2. What steps would have to occur before that goal became a reality?

   _____

   _____

   _____

   _____

   _____

   _____

3. What roadblocks stand in the way of you becoming that which your soul desires?

   Is there a path around these temporary objections? What is it?

   _____   _____

   _____   _____

   _____   _____

   _____   _____

   _____   _____

   _____   _____

> "I have a dream..."
>
> Martin Luther King, Jr.

When I Was Ten

Who Do You Want to Be?

*W*hen I was ten years old I won a Lions Club Boy-of-the-Month award. Men smiled at me with that "You're going places, son" look and my parents were thrilled. I was happy, too.

The Lions called the local newspaper and a reporter asked me what I wanted to do when I grew up. I said, "I want to travel around the world and help people get along with each other." It reads slightly pretentious; it was not meant that way.

During the last ten years I have traveled to eight hundred campuses in fifty states, five countries, three continents, and several islands to help people get along with each other. It was a childhood dream. Now it is a reality. Students write and tell me it is helping them, changing their lives. What do you want to do? Who do you want to be? What is your dream? Do not be afraid. Sometimes dreams come true.

Think not..."what do I want to do?..." Think "who do I want to be?" The job part will follow.

❖

Dream big; do not compromise willingly.

❖

You can be whatever you resolve yourself to be.

A Moment for Reflection
When I Was Ten

1. Can you recall a childhood event that sparks a current academic or vocational interest? Describe the experience:

   _____

   _____

   _____

   _____

   _____

2. What events or people shaped the person you are today?

   _____

   _____

   _____

   _____

   _____

3. Write down (for yourself) your secret dream: what do you hope for in your best case scenario?

   _____

   _____

   _____

   _____

   _____

> "I like the dreams of
> the future better
> than the history of
> the past."
>
> Thomas Jefferson

LESSON 8

Letting Go
You Can Go Home Again

I believe that an essential part of growing up, of successfully navigating through life's many transitions, is learning to let go. Of what?

- Of resentment of your parents for not being perfect.
- Of your brothers and sisters for hogging your parent's attention and all the awards.
- Of the fact that you didn't have brothers and sisters, and much, much more.

Let go of memories that cause you pain or remorse. Focus your energies on thoughts that give life rather than diminish it. You can go home again, but only if you will let your parents evolve into your friends. You are not perfect....Why should they be? Dream about your future. Let the history of your past be just that...history.

Keep your intention and desires on the future; you cannot change the past.

❖

Pay attention to the present; this is the field of play today.

❖

"Let go" of your pain, remorse, and regret. The sun will rise tomorrow!

A Moment for Reflection
Letting Go

1. If I could change one thing about my life, it would be:

    _____

    _____

    _____

    _____

    _____

2. The single most important thing I must learn to let go of is:

    _____

    _____

    _____

    _____

    _____

3. To let go I may need to: (Check as many as are appropriate.)
    ☐ Say I am sorry   ☐ Participate in a support group
    ☐ Learn to forgive   ☐ Read more on a certain topic
    ☐ Talk to a friend   ☐ Pray
    ☐ Talk to my parent(s)   ☐ Move to a better place for me
    ☐ See a counselor   ☐ Other _____

> "If you don't know
> where you are
> going to,
> you will end up
> somewhere else."
>
> **Lewis Carroll,
> Alice In Wonderland**

LESSON 9

A Good Map

Not Just Any Road Will Get You There

*Y*ou would never begin a journey to a far-off place without a good map. Entering a location where "strange customs prevail" would be difficult if not impossible without a chart, a map, a planned direction.

Why, then, begin your journey into the rest of your life without a map? Where can you get this map? Here are some ideas.

- Visit the Career Planning Center today.
- Update, or create, a resumé today.
- Seek out professionals in your field and ask them to be your mentor today.
- See your academic advisor today.
- Send five letters to prospective employers or graduate schools today.
  (Key word: <u>TODAY</u>) Then repeat tomorrow.

Not to decide is to decide. No choice is a choice. Create your life map with great care. No one will, or can, do this for you. Know where it is you are going. You may end up there.

Not just any road will get you there.
❖
Not to decide...is to decide.
❖
Prepare a good life map...in pencil or saved "on file" on a disc.

A Moment for Reflection
A Good Map

1. Draw a map of your life's travels to date:

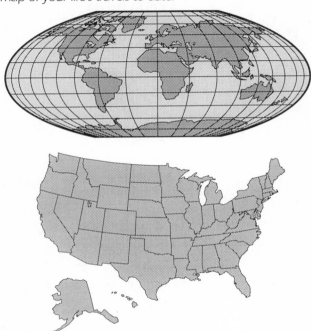

2. What patterns do you see? Are you well traveled? What influences have shaped your life map?

☐ Parents
☐ War
☐ Academics
☐ Siblings
☐ Divorce
☐ Sports
☐ Church, mosque, synagogue
☐ Alcohol, drugs, sex
☐ Other —————————

Your State

> "Live to learn and
> you will learn to live."
>
> Portuguese Proverb

L E S S O N   1 0

Commencement

Only the Beginning

*g*raduation day is right up there with all the great moments. The state championships, the prom, the initiation, the merit scholarship, the first collegiate acceptance letter. It is the crowning glory to a successful higher education experience.

It is, however, not called the ending. Or the climax. Or the grand finale. It is the commencement: meaning, the beginning. Just the start of many great things to come. It is only the beginning: your start.

If for one minute you believe that you now know everything you will need to know, then all your professors have failed their mighty task. As the information in the world doubles every three years and as eight thousand scientific articles are published every day, you will need to know more and be open to learning every day. Live to learn and you will become an interesting and employable individual. Learn to live to love to learn!

Commencement means to commence: to begin.

❖

Every day the rest of your life is a final exam.

❖

Learn to live to love to learn. (L^4!)

A Moment for Reflection
Commencement

1. How is the university commencement experience different from the high school experience?

_____

_____

_____

_____

2. Ask five graduating students what their plans are for next year.

STUDENT	PLAN	MAJOR/G.P.A.
_____	_____	_____
_____	_____	_____
_____	_____	_____
_____	_____	_____
_____	_____	_____
_____	_____	_____
_____	_____	_____

3. What are your "continuing education plans"?
   - ☐ Graduate school
   - ☐ Professional school
   - ☐ Work
   - ☐ Travel
   - ☐ Research
   - ☐ Language study
   - ☐ Study abroad
   - ☐ Summer study
   - ☐ Corporate training
   - ☐ Other _____

"You gain strength, courage, and confidence by every experience in which you really stop to look fear in the face....You must do the thing you think you cannot do."

Eleanor Roosevelt

LESSON 11

The Importance of Fear
The Great Motivator

*W*hile you may have nothing to fear but fear itself, leaving campus should at least merit a little consideration. The corporate ladder is much more confusing than the undergraduate catalog. Everyone in graduate school will be a survivor with a plan for his or her success. What to do?

Let fear move you. Feel the pressure that will one day soon push you out of the comfortable surroundings and into the next phase of your life. You will have to open the closet, check under the bed, and see what lurks in the darkness. There is no other way.

You have done many things others thought you could not do. Now you must do the thing you thought you could not do. Get up, gather your belongings and your memories, and head out into the world. Look fear in the face. It will blink!

Fear is a great motivator.
❖
Look your fear in the face.
❖
A life lived in fear is a life half lived.

A Moment for Reflection
The Importance of Fear

1. Identify three experiences or thoughts that frightened you as a child:

   (a) _____

   (b) _____

   (c) _____

2. Describe for yourself your most frightening personal experience:

   _____

   _____

   _____

   _____

   _____

3. What is your biggest fear about graduation? What do you plan to do to face your fear?

   _____

   _____

   _____

   _____

   _____

> "Four things
> come not back—
> the spoken word,
> the sped arrow,
> the past life, and
> the neglected
> opportunity."
>
> **Arabian Proverb**

The New Kid in Town

Starting Over Again

*M*y father once said, "Just when I learned all the answers, they changed all the questions." This was not his original thought, but I believe he was trying to tell me something. I was young and had all the answers, or so I thought.

What I am trying to tell you is that it does not matter one iota to your new employer or graduate school dean how much you have accomplished in the past or what victories were won in yesterday's races. You are new again, the rookie, a neophyte, and almost everyone believes you have more to learn than you may think.

Listen to them. Hold the quickly spoken word, pull back the defensive arrow. Once shot, it comes not back. Do not neglect this opportunity to start over and let the "experts" mentor you. You will be thankful.

A growing person is always new at something.

❖

Select a mentor and listen.

❖

Do not be afraid to start over.

A Moment for Reflection
The New Kid in Town

1. List all the times in school you have started over (i.e. new grade, new school, new major, etc.).

   _____

   _____

   _____

   _____

   _____

   _____

2. What was the most difficult period of transition for you? Why?

   _____

   _____

   _____

   _____

   _____

   _____

3. Give three pieces of advice to someone starting over at your university:

   (a) _____

   (b) _____

   (c) _____

> "Complacency is a far more dangerous attitude than outrage."
>
> Naomi Littlebear

LESSON 13

Making Informed Choices
Knowledge Is Power

*F*ive of my thirteen second-year Master's students did not have resumés ready during winter term. What were they waiting for? A resident assistant on my staff said, "I have to go to the library. I avoided it for four years, but I have to go for this class." Hmm....

If you have learned one thing I hope it is that you have learned to love to learn. Knowledge is power and power is choice. A meaningful life is a life filled with choices. "I hire attitude and communication," the CEO said. "I'll teach them the rest."

Do not become complacent with your learning. Lifelong learning will result in lifelong enjoyment, growth, and very likely, employment. Become outrageous in your search for knowledge and information. You will feel the power that knowledge brings and your choices will be informed ones.

Knowledge is power.

Sometimes we learn; sometimes we must unlearn or relearn.

Learning is a lifelong enterprise.

A Moment for Reflection
Making Informed Choices

1. Write down five things you are absolutely sure of:

    (a) _____

    (b) _____

    (c) _____

    (d) _____

    (e) _____

2. List your one unbending, absolutely held belief:

    _____

    _____

    _____

    _____

    _____

3. Check the following boxes where appropriate: Do you know...

    ☐ Your family history   ☐ What your moral principles are

    ☐ Your nation's history   ☐ Three scholars whose work is in your field

    ☐ What it takes to get   ☐ What the repayment schedule is on your
       hired in your field   student loans

KNOWLEDGE IS POWER!

"No man or woman,
even of the
humblest sort, can
really be strong,
gentle, pure, and
good without the
world being better
for it; without
somebody being
helped and
comforted by the
very existence of
that goodness."

Phillips Brooks

LESSON 14

The Education of Character

Lessons for Beginners

*L*ife is much more than possession and obsession. The kind of car you drive does <u>not</u> say a lot about the kind of person you are despite what the commercial says.

Martin Buber wrote, "Education worthy of the name is essentially education of character." Key words of character include <u>trustworthy</u>, <u>caring</u>, <u>gentle</u>, <u>good</u>, <u>well</u>, <u>committed</u>, <u>honest</u>, and <u>promise keeper</u>. How do you and I measure up? Can we be trusted to say what we mean and do what we say? Will we admit our mistakes when, <u>not if</u>, we make them?

If we are men and women of character, then the world is a better place. Someone will be helped, someone will be comforted.

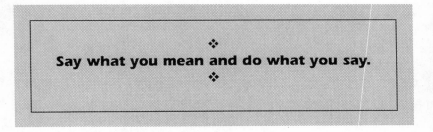

❖
Say what you mean and do what you say.
❖

A Moment for Reflection
The Education of Character

1. List your five most precious or valuable earthly possessions:

    (a) _____

    (b) _____

    (c) _____

    (d) _____

    (e) _____

2. List them again:

    _____

    _____

    _____   Which one of these is more
                                          valuable than health? Your
    _____   family? Your friends?

    _____   **?**

3. Give an example of a time when you stood up for what you believe
    and it cost you something or someone:

    _____

    _____

    _____

    _____

    _____

    _____

> "Don't compromise
> yourself. You are all
> you've got."
>
> Janis Joplin

Goals and Objectives

Set Them, Meet Them,
Enjoy Them

*D*o you do long-range planning?" they asked the chairman of Matushita Corporation. His response: "Yes." Their next question: "How long is your long-range planning?" His answer: "Five hundred years." Everyone laughed except the chairman of one of the world's largest companies.

Set short, medium, and long-term goals. Under each heading outline specific objectives to reach those goals. Share your lists with a trusted and wise mentor. Accept his or her feedback. Make adjustments and go for it! When you reach a goal, pause, reflect, and enjoy the accomplishment, then set new goals. "Do your job, then step back," writes Master Lao-Tzu.

Do not compromise yourself and your ethics. Your word is your bond. Your honor, your badge. Do the right thing. You are, after all, all you've really got!

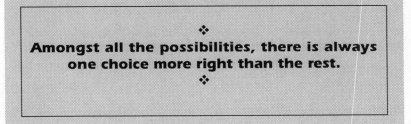

❖
Amongst all the possibilities, there is always one choice more right than the rest.
❖

A Moment for Reflection
Goals and Objectives

1. Where do you want to be:

    (a) In 6 months? _____

    (b) In 2 years? _____

    (c) In 10 years? _____

    (d) In 25 years? _____

2. What is the goal you have held for the longest time that you have achieved?

    _____

    _____

    _____

    _____

    _____

3. Looking ahead, what specific objectives can you state that will help you reach your goals in question #1 above?

    6-month goal's objective: _____

    2-year goal's objective: _____

    10-year goal's objective: _____

    25-year goal's objective: _____

"You will make all
kinds of mistakes;
but as long as you
are generous and
true, and also fierce,
you cannot hurt the
world or even
seriously distress her.
She was made to be
wooed and won by
youth."

Winston Churchill

L E S S O N 1 6

20/20 Vision

You Cannot Go Forward Looking Backward

*M*y mother had a tough life. Her mother died during my mom's infancy, she was the last child of four to be adopted, married twice, lost my dad three months into her pregnancy, and died in poor health.

She lived her last years in regret for a past filled with hurtful events out of her control, and choices made that resulted in pain. She feared the future, especially death, and worried constantly about what would go wrong tomorrow.

You can live only in the present. Your past mistakes are just that...past. Focus your vision on today. Surely dream of tomorrow, but see today as the recipient of your energy. You cannot go forward looking back. Look to today. Watch your footing here and now. The mountain ahead will be there when you arrive.

> **Pay attention...
> to your present.**
> ❖
> **Pay intention...
> to your future.**

A Moment for Reflection
20/20 Vision

1. What are the three biggest mistakes or regrets that you have?

    (a) _____

    (b) _____

    (c) _____

2. Utilizing the Past, the Present, and the Future, divide the circle into percentages of time you spend thinking about each of these areas (must equal 100%).

100% OF YOUR TIME

3. Identify one thing that you can do today to move closer to your goal of graduation, graduate school, or employment:

    _____

    _____

    _____

    _____

    _____

    _____

"The final test of a leader is that he [she] leaves behind him [her] in other men [women] the will to carry on....The genius of a good leader is to leave behind him [her] a situation which common sense, without grace of genius, can deal with successfully."

Walter Lippmann

Leaders Are Risk Takers

Beware the Kitty Hawk People

*I*t will never fly." "Yep, never will get off the ground." "Uh-huh...if God wanted us to fly we'd have wings." You can imagine many of the doubters on the beach at Kitty Hawk, North Carolina, giving their expert opinions on why the Wright Brothers were doomed. Then, the short flight. Now, the stars.

Leaders are risk takers who take reasonable, well-thought-out chances to reach their dreams. Leaders listen, delegate, and inspire others to share their vision. The Wright Brothers did not envision the space shuttle, but their dream opened the window and let the bird fly.

There will always be Kitty Hawk people raining on your parade. Consider their objections, fine tune your vision, and set sail. Leadership is a lonely and risky enterprise. Great are the rewards for dreams well dreamt.

❖
Others will always tell you what to do. This is conventional wisdom. Sometimes they are wrong so follow your heart.
❖

A Moment for Reflection
Leaders Are Risk Takers

1. Name the five greatest leaders you know or have read about:

    (a) _____

    (b) _____

    (c) _____

    (d) _____

    (e) _____

2. Now list these leaders' characteristics: What did they <u>do</u> that made them a leader in your opinion?

    LEADER   CHARACTERISTIC(S)

    (a) _____   _____

    (b) _____   _____

    (c) _____   _____

    (d) _____   _____

    (e) _____   _____

3. Who is your mentor? (If you don't have at least one...get one!) Who is guiding and teaching you about leadership?

    _____   _____

    _____   _____

    _____   _____

    _____   _____

> "Life is either a
> daring adventure
> or nothing."
>
> Helen Keller

Victims and Directors

Choose, Accept, Direct

*O*ur country has developed into a culture of excuse, a cult of victimology, a nation of victims packing pistols, legal briefs, and a huge chip on our collective shoulder. This is one bit of insanity that must be stopped.

We have all been hurt, and at times victimized, even traumatized. Welcome to life! It isn't fair, even remotely just. It just is and we must grow up soon, as individuals and as citizens. We must overcome our past and our limitations, and our victimizations and become "response able."

We are the directors of our fate, not victims of some cosmic joke. We must choose, accept the consequences of those choices, and direct ourselves into better situations. No one can nor will do this for us. Life is an adventure and a daring one. Make it something; something special! Take responsibility for your life work-in-progress.

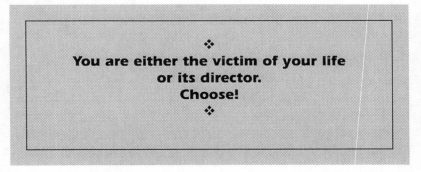

❖
**You are either the victim of your life
or its director.
Choose!**
❖

A Moment for Reflection
Victims and Directors

1. List all groups to which you belong that would qualify you for membership in the cult of victimology (i.e., in my case, Adult Child of an Alcoholic, Deceased Parents, Abused Child).*

   _____   _____

   _____   _____

   _____   _____

   _____   _____

2. What steps have you taken to get out of your victim status?
   ☐ Personal reflection   ☐ Confronting person(s)
   ☐ Help from friends   ☐ Personal decision to "get well"
   ☐ Professional counseling   ☐ Prayer
   ☐ Forgiving   ☐ Other _____

3. What will you do today to begin your own healing process? What will you do to begin to take charge of your life?

   _____

   _____

   _____

   _____

   * Many self-help groups are instrumental in helping individuals get over feelings of victimization and on with their lives.

> "No choice is a
> choice too."
>
> **Yiddish Proverb**

Tonic or Toxic

Life or Death

*I*f someone takes toxins into their system, then the body will be poisoned and become sick or die. Taking a tonic into the body, one feels relief from indigestion or pain. So it is with your spirit.

Take into yourself those ideas that add meaning, hope, and joy to your life. These tonics will ease the stress of modern living. Refuse to "digest" toxic thoughts or ideas that poison the soul.

Choose life; that is, choose to live fully, adding zest and sparkle to everyone you touch. Do not poison yourself or others with negativism. Energy creates energy, positivism breeds optimism. Do not listen to your detractors or the dark voices of doom. With all its problems, it is a wonderful life. And brief—enjoy it!

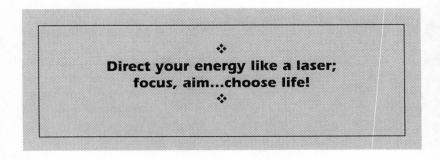

❖
**Direct your energy like a laser;
focus, aim...choose life!**
❖

A Moment for Reflection
Tonic or Toxic

1. Describe a situation in your life that could have been seen by you as tonic or toxic: an upper or downer. Choose one in which you gave yourself or someone else the benefit of the doubt and things turned out for the best.

   _____

   _____

   _____

   _____

   _____

2. Describe a situation or event that you remember in which you chose the downside....What was the result?

   _____

   _____

   _____

   _____

   _____

3. Choose now to describe your experience at the university in the most glowing terms possible. Be positive!

   _____

   _____

   _____

   _____

> "We don't see things
> as they are, we see
> things as we are."
>
> Anaïs Nin

Half Full, Half Empty

*The Glass, the Steak,
and the Mushroom*

*L*ife reveals three kinds of people. We see the glass as half full, not half empty. Some see it half empty and long for what's missing. The third group knows the glass is half empty and further, they don't like what's in it. Join us—we are happier!

The prime cut of beef is either a filet mignon with shitake mushrooms or a piece of dead cow with fungus. Which is more appealing to you? It is really the same, but the way we choose to see and define our world directly impacts our ability to live in that world happily and peacefully with one another.

What we see in the world reveals much of what we feel about ourselves. See beauty, grace, and love. Then you will be these things.

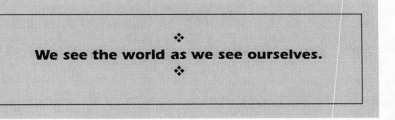

❖
We see the world as we see ourselves.
❖

A Moment for Reflection
Half Full, Half Empty

1. "Language creates reality." Do you believe this? Why? Why not?

    _____

    _____

    _____

    _____

    _____

2. Please describe the following things positively, then negatively
    (i.e., filet mignon with mushroom versus dead cow with fungus).

ITEM	DESCRIPTION (+)	DESCRIPTION (-)
(a) Grilled swordfish	_____	_____
(b) New York City	_____	_____
(c) The U.S.A.	_____	_____
(d) Your university	_____	_____
(e) Your future	_____	_____

3. Is your glass:

    ☐ Half full

    ☐ Half empty

> "Getting ahead in a profession requires avid faith in yourself....That is why some people with mediocre talent, but with great inner drive, go much further than people with vastly superior talent."
>
> **Sophia Loren**

LESSON 21

On Becoming a Professional

Professional or Functionary

*E*very profession has a set of standards and best practices that guides the members' behavior. Mission statements and standards for ethical conduct move a set of tasks from functions to professional responsibilities.

A professional is a person who takes valued purpose and transforms it into tasks, processes, and duties. A functionary does a job. Little value, little care. Which way do you think will result in self-satisfaction?

You will spend one half of your awake time at your profession and some hours of your sleep time dreaming about it. Any function can become a profession in the mind and heart of the doer. Believe in yourself and focus your inner drive. No one can make you a functionary without your consent. No one can make you a professional without your avid commitment.

> ❖
> **Being a professional requires a talent, a decision, and an iron will.**
> ❖

A Moment for Reflection
On Becoming a Professional

1. List the jobs you have held to this point in your life.

   _____

   _____

   _____

   _____

   _____

2. Were these functionary or professional positions? Why?

   _____

   _____

   _____

   _____

   _____

3. Do you take yourself seriously enough to become a professional at whatever you do?

   ☐ YES   ☐ NO

> "We can do no
> great things—only
> small things with
> great love."
>
> Mother Teresa

On Becoming a Contributor

Making a Difference

*W*e have done you a grave disservice at the college or university you are attending by selling you the "leadership myth." Imagine an army full of generals with no soldiers. Consider a company stocked with middle management leadership, but no one moving inventory in the warehouse, no one stocking products on the shelves.

Forget about leadership. Focus your energy on contributorship. You will occasionally lead, but you can always contribute. Every day, every hour, make a conscious decision to put in your best effort: to cooperate, communicate, commit yourself to the accomplishment of a common task.

While you are doing small things with great love, others will recognize your daily contribution and you will emerge as a leader. Let others sing your praises and move you to the front. Ask yourself, "What can I do today to contribute to the betterment of myself, the company, my city, state, nation, and world."

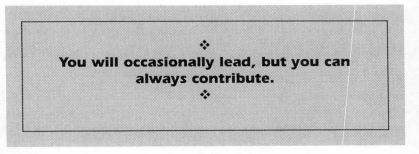

❖
You will occasionally lead, but you can always contribute.
❖

A Moment for Reflection
On Becoming a Contributor

1.   Define "leadership":

_____

_____

_____

_____

_____

2.   Describe your leadership and contributorship experiences during college:

_____

_____

_____

_____

_____

3.   Write a definition of contributorship:

_____

_____

_____

_____

_____

> "Love grows by
> service."
>
> Charlotte Perkins Gilman

Do Your Job,
Then Step Back

*You Are More
Than Your Work*

*W*ouldn't it be wonderful if when two people met for the first time they would ask, "Who are you?" rather than, "What do you do?" Ideally our work is an outgrowth of who we are, but we clearly are more than the job or profession we do to pay life's way.

The Tao tells us to do our work then step back. The implication is that we should take time to live. We should work to live, not live to work. Our work is no compensation for the absence of friends and family. John Wooden said that three things mattered: family, faith, and profession. What is important to you?

When we die our possessions will be of little comfort. Our friends and family and children will ease our fear. Take care of the things that really count. Serve your clients, but understand that love grows in service to your friends and family.

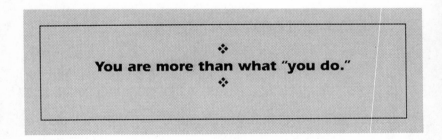

❖

You are more than what "you do."

❖

A Moment for Reflection
Do Your Job, Then Step Back

1. I tell my children that three things are important:

    ☐ Family

    ☐ Faith

    ☐ Friends

    What is important to you? _____

    _____

    _____

2. Do you believe that your job is the greatest indication of who you are?

    ☐ YES   ☐ NO

    Why?_____

    _____

    _____

3. Of your total time, what percentage is spent on:

    ____% your job   ____% your studies ____% your friends

    ____% your family   ____% your faith   ____% your service to
    others

"The ultimate measure of a man is not where he stands in the moments of comfort and convenience, but where he stands in times of challenge and controversy."

Martin Luther King, Jr.

Humility 101

"You've Got a Lot to Learn, Willy!"

*I*t was at my fortieth birthday party that I realized how little I really truly know for certain. Why, when I was half my age I was so sure about so much. I lectured my parents about child-centered marriages, analyzed Washington politics with great clarity, and could run my university much better than the president and administration botching the job.

Now, as Billy Joel concurs, I see "increasing shades of gray." The "sure" frighten me. Those who justify the means by the end are dangerous to a free mind or to society. Life is not predictable, we are not in control, and we clearly are working without a net. You are here because your ancestors took "reasonable" risks.

Humility 101: Accept yourself and your role and see yourself connecting to a greater whole. My father said, "Willy, you've got a lot to learn." Take a stand, but have a fall-back position. Bend, but do not break. The bamboo survives the horrible hurricane; the great oak shatters.

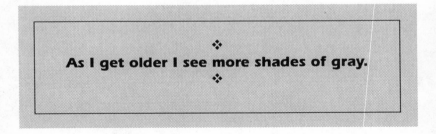

❖
As I get older I see more shades of gray.
❖

A Moment for Reflection
Humility 101

1. Which of the following characterizes your lifestyle:

   ☐ the oak tree

   ☐ the bamboo plant

   ☐ the sage brush

   Why?_____

   _____

   _____

   _____

   _____

2. What is the greatest lesson of humility that life has taught you?

   _____

   _____

   _____

   _____

   _____

3. Think about this:
   Be tentative in your analysis and judgment. In five years time, this point in your life may look as silly as a point five years ago looks to you now. **We are more than what we have been, and not yet all that we will be.**

> "When in doubt, tell
> the truth."
>
> Mark Twain

Professional Ethics

On Being Trustworthy

*Y*our personal sense of self and professional reputation will both be greatly enhanced if you do one thing: tell the truth. Before you make a decision, consider four important questions.

1. Why am I doing this?

2. What is the law or company policy?

3. What are the probable consequences of my behavior?

4. What are my moral principles regarding my decisions?

When I asked a senior vice president of State Farm Insurance what he thought was the most desirable quality of employees, he said, "Loyalty." You should be loyal to your principles, your beliefs, your family, yourself, and your company. Be a professional who says what she or he means, and does what he or she says. Tell the truth and do the right thing. And remember, there is always one choice more right than the others.

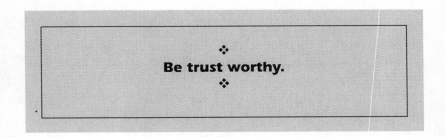

❖
Be trust worthy.
❖

A Moment for Reflection
Professional Ethics

1. Why have you chosen your major?

    _____

    _____

    _____

    _____

    _____

2. What are the consequences of your choice?

    _____

    _____

    _____

    _____

    _____

3. How does your professional path fit in with who you see yourself to
    be? Is your vocational path a logical extension of yourself? Explain.

    _____

    _____

    _____

    _____

    _____

"If folks can learn to be racist, then they can learn to be antiracist. If being a sexist ain't genetic, then, dad gum, people can learn about gender equality."

Johnnetta Betsch Cole

Color, Gender, Age, and Prejudice

Keep Your Eyes on the Prize

*W*atching my children play with other children of different shapes, sizes, ages, abilities, sexes, and colors has taught me that prejudice is a learned behavior. If someone is learning it, then others must be teaching it.

The workplace and graduate school are riddled with outdated attitudes about the importance of age, color, and gender. Laws have been enacted, but you cannot force equality down citizens' throats with litigious forks and bigotous knives.

Treat other people like you want to be treated. Unlearn unhealthy attitudes and focus on positive, tolerant, and affirming behavior with your coworkers. Keep your eyes on your long-range goals and objectives. Hate and prejudice sap precious energy that would best be expended someplace else. Learn to get along!

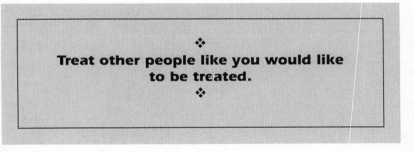

❖

Treat other people like you would like to be treated.

❖

A Moment for Reflection
Color, Gender, Age, and Prejudice

1. This is my most closely held stereotype about another race or group:

   _____

   _____

   _____

   _____

   _____

2. I reached this conclusion about these people because:

   _____

   _____

   _____

   _____

   _____

3. This year I will work to make better relationships with:

   _____

   _____

   _____

   Because: _____

   _____

   _____

> "To be successful,
> the first thing to do
> is fall in love with
> your work."
>
> Sister Mary Lauretta

A Ph.D. in Life

Respect Life Experience

*T*he most frightening characteristic of a university or college education is the arrogance with which it is delivered and the mindlessness with which it is received. How many of you have had professors who said, "The reason this is important is because _____," and "It will assist you in obtaining employment by _____." If not, are you really prepared for life after college?

How many student friends did you have who were third-year undeclared majors, or seniors, fifth year, who had no resumé, no plan, no clue? No future!

A Ph.D. in Life is what you receive from the University of Experience. College sets the table; life is the feast. Do not let your B.S. or M.B.A. cloud your vision. There is much to learn and you will learn it more quickly if you respect the life experience of the people with whom you are working. There are a great many bellboys with B.A.s.

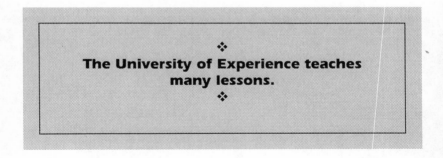

❖
The University of Experience teaches many lessons.
❖

A Moment for Reflection
A Ph.D. in Life

1. Who are the brightest, most informed, most caring people you know
    who did <u>not</u> attend college?

    _____

    _____

    _____

    _____

    _____

2. What lessons did these people teach you?

    _____

    _____

    _____

    _____

    _____

3. What is the single most important teaching you have received
    outside of the university?

    _____

    _____

    _____

    _____

    _____

> "Be good to
> yourself, be excellent
> to others and do
> everything with
> love."
>
> John Wolf

Can't Buy Me Love

Money, Credit, and Debt

*g*t might be expected that with an immediate post-graduation job-related influx of capital that you would want to pick up some goodies you resisted during school. Even a graduate teaching assistantship can seem like a windfall profit.

If credit card companies suddenly find you a good-looking customer, what might this tell you? If you get in the habit of overspending now it will diminish the effects of your hard work over the next ten years. Use credit for transportation to work, if needed. Use it to finance additional training, or education needed for advancement, for a home, or for your family.

But hear this: Do not get over your head in debt. Many relationships are lost over money fights. Be smart. Be good to yourself. Be excellent to others. Love!

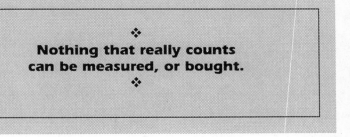

❖
**Nothing that really counts
can be measured, or bought.**
❖

A Moment for Reflection
Can't Buy Me Love

1. What possessions do you currently <u>not</u> own that you would desire, capital notwithstanding?

_____

_____

_____

_____

_____

2. Do you really need these items? Or want them?

_____

_____

_____

_____

3. List your debts and assets. Are you currently in the black or the red? Plus or minus?

Debts	Assets	Net

"If only I could so
live and so serve the
world that after me
there should never
again be birds in
cages."

Isak Dinesen

L E S S O N 2 9

Take Care of the Temple
Body, Mind, and Spirit

*Y*our body is the temple that "houses" your spirit and potential and you must take an hour a day for temple maintenance and upkeep. Here is a sure prescription for stress reduction:

Exercise one half hour daily,
and follow this with one half hour of:
>**Meditation,**
>**Contemplation,**
>or **Prayer**—pick one.

If you put your bird—your spirit—in a cage, then it will never soar. The cage may be made of stress, damaging competition (as opposed to healthy competition), alcohol abuse, or drug use. Destroy the cage. Clean out the temple. Stephen Covey says rightly, "sharpen your saw." You are your product and you are what you are selling. Take care of the goods!

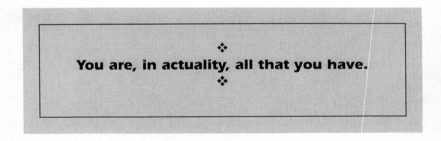

❖
You are, in actuality, all that you have.
❖

A Moment for Reflection
Take Care of the Temple

1. Describe your weekly workout schedule:

   M _____

   T _____

   W _____

   Th _____

   F _____

   S _____

   Sun _____

2. How many hours a week do you:

   ☐ Pray

   ☐ Meditate

   ☐ Sit in reflective silence

3. What are the ways that you "Sharpen Your Saw"?*

   _____

   _____

   _____

   _____

   *Stephen Covey

> "Eternity is not something that begins after you are dead. It is going on all the time. We are in it now."
>
> Charlotte Perkins Gilman

LESSON 30

The Spirit Journey

The Road Is Long, the Well Is Deep

*O*ne of the main reasons I volunteer time to serve as a campus minister is that I am trying to help students get in the habit of worshiping God. In community with other students and faculty, one hopes that they will take God with them to the workplace or graduate school.

Your concepts of the Eternal will be as varied as your skin color or career plans. This is as it should be. Which of us knows exactly what the Eternal is like? Who of us speaks directly for God?

All I want you to think of is that God is, much as air is. You may choose not to believe in air, but it nonetheless fills your lungs. Recognize that life is a spiritual journey and the wellspring of the Eternal is deep. You do not go out from college alone. I really believe this!

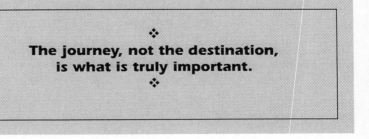

❖
**The journey, not the destination,
is what is truly important.**
❖

A Moment for Reflection
The Spirit Journey

1. Do you believe in God? The Great Spirit? Yahweh? Allah? The Eternal Thou? A Higher Power?

    _____

    _____

    _____

2. What is your explanation for the origins of our universe? Your life?

    _____

    _____

    _____

    _____

    _____

    _____

3. Is your journey a spirit journey?

    _____

    _____

    _____

    _____

    _____

> "In the struggle for justice, the only reward is the opportunity to be in the struggle. You can't expect that you're going to have it tomorrow. You just have to keep working on it."
>
> Frederick Douglass

LESSON 31

The Problem or the Solution
The High Road

*L*ife is a struggle, first for survival, then for purpose, finally for justice and equality, and ultimately love. If you are not part of the solution to our world's problems and ills, then you are likely part of the problem.

Leadership is service. Integrity is rare. Do not choose to be the rule; be the exception. Stand up for what is right; do not take the unethical shortcut. Keep working on it until you get it right. I was not the brightest guy in my graduating class, but I have outworked a bunch of them.

Take the high road. It leads to a better future for you, your family, friends...everyone! Be remembered as a just and ethical person, a champion of equality, a leader who served. Take the high road!

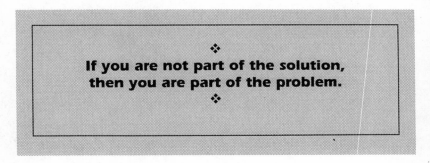

❖
**If you are not part of the solution,
then you are part of the problem.**
❖

A Moment for Reflection
The Problem or the Solution

1. What is the greatest injustice in the United States today?

   _____

   _____

   _____

   _____

   _____

2. Have you contributed to this injustice?

   _____

   _____

   _____

   _____

   _____

3. What are you doing to address and redress the problem?

   _____

   _____

   _____

   _____

   _____

> "The dogmas of the
> quiet past are
> inadequate to the
> stormy present."
>
> Abraham Lincoln

Good Advice

Listen to What the People Say

*K*evin Costner once said, "People will always tell you what to do with your life. This is called conventional wisdom. Sometimes they are wrong, so follow your heart." Listen to what people say, run it by your heart, and then act accordingly with intent and an acceptance of responsibility.

Do not throw out the baby with the bathwater. **Translation:** Just because an idea is old doesn't necessarily mean it's bad. We live in a death-denying, youth-at-all-costs society. Be wise enough to glean the best of the old and the best of the new.

Listen to those around you, then make up your mind. Seek good advice and counsel from a diversity of sources. No man or woman is self-made. The stormy present demands the wise counsel of age and the enthusiasm of youth.

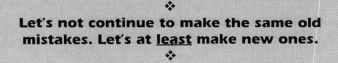

❖
Let's not continue to make the same old mistakes. Let's at least make new ones.
❖

A Moment for Reflection
Good Advice

1. A piece of good advice a professor gave to me is:

   _____

   _____

   _____

   _____

   _____

2. My mother/father once said:

   _____

   _____

   _____

   _____

3. My own most original insight is:

   _____

   _____

   _____

   _____

> "Never before have
> we had so little time
> in which to do so
> much."
>
> Franklin Delano Roosevelt

25,000 Days
Your Life Time

*W*hen you strip life to its barest form, it is seventy-five years times three hundred and sixty-five days for a total of approximately 25,000 days. Some lives are longer, some will end much sooner. My real father got forty-one years, my step dad sixty-six. My mom died at seventy-one. Katie Lyn Marcum lived 48 hours. How much time will you and I have?

You must continue, or begin to:
>Live life passionately,
>with great purpose,
>as if you don't have
>all the time in the world.

Because you don't! 25,000 days. The day I realized that I had spent 14,000 of my 25,000 days was the day I quit wasting time. The saddest thing for me to see as an educator is witnessing students who believe that their lives have not started yet when 6,500 of their days have already gone.

Get busy. Never have you had so much to do in so little time. Make your 25,000 days an adventure. Life is a "one ticket ride." One time through the line. Use your days wisely. Today is the day to choose to live...fully! This is your lifetime, your one time. Don't miss it.

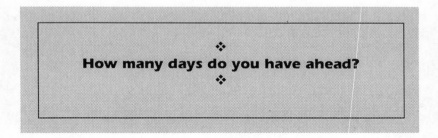

❖
How many days do you have ahead?
❖

A Moment for Reflection
25,000 Days

1. How old are you?

   _____

2. What is your age times 365? Add the days since your last birthday.

   _____

3. Subtract that total (from question #2 above) from 25,000.
   Approximately how many days do you have ahead?

   _____

Epilogue

The Three Stumbling Blocks

*Y*ou have likely seen the devastating effects of sex, alcohol, and drugs on several of your friends, brothers or sisters, or roommates during your campus tenure. I want you to remember that the acronym for these three stumbling blocks is:

> "It has been said that whenever you mention alcohol in our society people either get mad or thirsty."
>
> **Philip L. Hansen,**
> **The Afflicted and**
> **the Affected**

S ex   S.A.D.—and sad is what it will
A lcohol   be if your future is crippled
D rugs   because of any of these.

Please abstain from sex or practice safer sex. Respect yourself and your partner. Choose not to drink alcohol or practice low- or no-risk drinking. Consult the alcohol abuse prevention specialists for your campus for clear analysis regarding your drinking habits if you even mildly suspect you have a problem. And remember, if you have problems when you drink, then you are a problem drinker. Finally, no drugs! Clearly alcohol is a drug, though societally acceptable in moderate doses. I mean no coke, no crystal, no 'shrooms, no heroin. Your future will be severely crippled by a drug conviction.

Marijuana and other drugs are not the same as alcohol in the eyes of the state and if you doubt me on this, check out the 1990 Drug Free Campus and Community Act. Your future job may depend on you knowing it and living by it.

Your future is bright and can only be dimmed by dependence or addiction to sex, alcohol, and other drugs. Jim Matthews of Keene State College in New Hampshire, in a brilliant speech entitled, "I'll Quit After College...," reveals that fifty percent of heavy drinkers do not quit after college. Behavior once accepted at the residence hall or fraternity is not tolerated in the corporate board room of the twenty-first century. Too much is at stake, the market too competitive to make room for abuse.

Be smart. Be safe. Be alive. God speed and best wishes to you! Write when you get work!

The Meaning of Success

I do not want your life to be a galactic vortex of disappointment. I am afraid if you let the advertising-driven media teach you the meaning of success then you will never be happy. "The kind of car you drive says a lot about the kind of person you are." NO, IT DOESN'T! It says a lot about how much money you have to spend on transportation. "Who says you can't have it all?" I DO. No one has it all, except the man or woman who is no longer afraid to be himself or herself and is one who is at peace with his or her Maker. Success, then, is not about the accumulation of toys, goods, or paper money. Success is about service, character, integrity, honesty, loyalty, commitment, truthfulness, being trustworthy...doing your best for yourself, your family, your friends, community, state, province, nation, and world.

> "Success is the peace of mind that comes from knowing you did the best you were capable of doing and you are the only one that will ever know that."
>
> **John Wooden,
> UCLA Head Coach,
> Retired
> 10 National NCAA Championships,
> 7 in a row,
> 4 with undefeated seasons**

You can believe me or you can believe a lot of people trying to sell you something. All I am trying to sell you on is yourself, on being and doing your best. Listen to your own drummer; hear your own voice.

Please do not become a shallow reflection of values that are not your own. Take responsibility for your chapter of the world. Write your section of the book of life with dignity and integrity. Take the high road, the road to success.

Ultimately, and finally, you will be the only person who knows if you did your best anyway. Lincoln was wrong when he said you cannot fool all the people all the time. The only person you really cannot fool is yourself. The man or woman looking back at you in the mirror is the one you must be honest with. Do not become a dim reflection of your true self.

Be a success.

> "The only person in life you cannot fool for long is yourself."
>
> **Will Keim**

The Island of I, The Sea of We

*T*here is a great myth in America about the self-made man or woman. While myths are not inherently false, this one is! There is <u>no</u> such thing as a self-made person. We are conceived by two other persons, taught by other persons, and finally mentored and tutored by people who help us on our way.

> "We cannot live for ourselves alone."
>
> **Vernon E. Jordan, Jr.**

Do not be "an island of I" in "the sea of we." Be a team player, cooperate with others, and let people help you. An island can be equally lonely and isolated. Allow yourself to swim freely in the sea of humanity.

It is impossible to live for ourselves alone. We exist only in our relationships with others. Do not strand yourself in out-of-the-way locations where help cannot reach you if you need it. Be the kind of person who easily disperses the credit for your accomplishments. Your humility will be perceived by others as a virtue. Indeed, it is a virtue!

The Culture of Excuse:
The Cult of Victimology

It would seem that everyone has an excuse for their behavior based upon a rough childhood, psychological or sexual abuse, or socio-economic driven poverty or divorce.

I just don't buy it. As a child who never knew his father, was raised in an alcoholic home, and was sexually molested at age eight, I affirm the following:

> **I was victimized, but that was then, and this is now.**

"All humanity is one undivided and indivisible family, and each one of us is responsible for the misdeeds of all the others."

Gandhi

You may choose to be the victim of your life or the director. Be the director of your life's play. Leave the culture of excuse; accept responsibility for what happens to you. No more blaming or whining. Do not be a member of the cult of victimology.

You can overcome any disability that you are willing to acknowledge, face, and seek assistance with. We are one undivided and indivisible family. One people, many tribes. Join us!

Remember Your ABC's

"Never doubt
that a small
group of
thoughtful
committed
citizens can
change the
world; indeed,
it's the only thing
that ever has."

Margaret Mead

A **ccept responsibility for your life.**

B **uild bridges between yourself and others.**

C **ommit yourself to excellence**

"Every now and then I think about my own death, and I think about my own funeral.... If you get someone to deliver the eulogy, tell them not to talk too long. Tell them not to mention that I have a Nobel Peace Prize....Tell them not to mention that I have three or four hundred other awards....I'd like for somebody to say that day that Martin Luther King, Jr., tried to love somebody....

"Say that I was a drum major for justice. Say that I was a drum major for peace. That I was a drum major for righteousness.... I won't have any money to leave behind. I won't have the fine and luxurious things of life to leave behind. But I just want to leave a committed life behind."

Martin Luther King, Jr.

What will they say about us?

Appendix

Reference to Lesson 1 on page 5

3. **Checklist**: Things to accomplish before graduation and "Life After College." Put a check in the box next to the items you have accomplished:

☐ Visit to career planning center
☐ Resumé
☐ Cover letter
☐ Contact college alumni
☐ Work in desired field
☐ Graduate school application
☐ Graduate school acceptance
☐ Check registrar's office to insure accurate credit count
☐ Cap and gown
☐ Graduation announcements
☐ Graduation tickets
☐ Letters or gifts of congratulations to close friends
☐ Thank yous to parent(s), guardian(s), grandparent(s)
☐ Follow-up on all rejection letters—(What could I have done to make myself a better candidate)
☐ Contact national Greek letter group (if applicable) for alumni list in field
☐ Contact parents' business associates/colleagues
☐ Arrange for move to new locale or home
☐ Forwarding address to university or college
☐ Forwarding address to bank/credit union
☐ Forwarding address to post office
☐ Assess moving costs
☐ Pause to reflect on my accomplishments

Sources

Light One Candle: Quotes for Hope and Action.
Compiled by Arrington Chambliss, Wayne Meisel, and
Maura Wolf. Peter Pauper Press, Inc., White Plains, NY.
1991.

Alcoholism: The Afflicted and the Affected. Philip
Hansen. Park Print, Minneapolis, MN. 1980.

The Education of Character: Lessons for Beginners. Will
Keim. Harcourt Brace College Publishers. 1995.

Between Man & Man. Martin Buber. Macmillan, NY.
1926.

Spirit Journey. Will Keim. Chalice Press, St. Louis, MO.
1995.